LESSON PLANNING FOR TEACHERS

CASSELL

Other titles in the Cassell Education series

P. Ainley: *Young People Leaving Home*

P. Ainley and M. Corney: *Training for the Future: The Rise and Fall of the Manpower Services Commission*

G. Antonouris and J. Wilson: *Equal Opportunities in Schools: New Dimensions in Topic Work*

M. Barber: *Education in the Capital*

L. Bash and D. Coulby: *The Education Reform Act: Competition and Control*

D. E. Bland: *Managing Higher Education*

M. Booth, J. Furlong and M. Wilkin: *Partnership in Initial Teacher Training*

M. Bottery: *The Morality of the School*

G. Claxton: *Being a Teacher: A Positive Approach to Change and Stress*

G. Claxton: *Teaching to Learn: A Direction for Education*

D. Coffey: *Schools and Work: Developments in Vocational Education*

D. Coulby and L. Bash: *Contradiction and Conflict: The 1988 Education Act in Action*

D. Coulby and S. Ward (eds): *The Primary Core National Curriculum*

L. B. Curzon: *Teaching in Further Education* (4th edition)

P. Daunt: *Meeting Disability: A European Response*

J. Freeman: *Gifted Children Growing Up*

J. Lynch: *Education for Citizenship in a Multicultural Society*

J. Nias, G. Southworth and R. Yeomans: *Staff Relationships in the Primary School*

A. Orton: *Learning Mathematics* (2nd edition)

R. Ritchie (ed.): *Profiling in Primary Schools: a Handbook for Teachers*

A. Rogers: *Adults Learning for Development*

B. Spiecker and R. Straughan (eds): *Freedom and Indoctrination in Education: International Perspectives*

A. Stables: *An Approach to English*

R. Straughan: *Beliefs, Behaviour and Education*

M. Styles, E. Bearne and V. Watson (eds): *After Alice: Exploring Children's Literature*

S. Tann: *Developing Language in the Primary School*

H. Thomas: *Education Costs and Performance*

H. Thomas with G. Kirkpatrick and E. Nicholson: *Financial Delegation and the Local Management of Schools*

D. Thyer: *Mathematical Enrichment Exercises: A Teacher's Guide*

D. Thyer and J. Maggs: *Teaching Mathematics to Young Children* (3rd Edition)

W. Tulasiewicz and C.-Y. To: *World Religions and Educational Practice*

M. Watts: *The Science of Problem-Solving*

M. Watts (ed.) : *Science in the National Curriculum*

J. Wilson: *A New Introduction to Moral Education*

S. Wolfendale et al. (eds): *The Profession and Practice of Educational Psychology: Future Directions*

Lesson Planning for Teachers

Peter D. John

Cassell Educational Limited
Villiers House
41/47 Strand
London WC2N 5JE

387 Park Avenue South
New York
NY 10016-8810

First published 1993

British Library Cataloguing-in-publication Data
A catalogue record for this book is available from the British Library.

Library of Congress Cataloging-in-Publication Data
John, Peter.
    Lesson planning for teachers / Peter John
        p.   cm. -- (Cassell education)
    Includes bibliographical references and index.
    ISBN 0-304-32625-9 : $ 20
    1. Lesson planning--United States. 2. Classroom Management-
United States.   I. Title. II. Series.
LB 1027.4.J64 1993
    371.3'028--dc.20   92-42793
                                            CIP

ISBN 0-304-32625-9 (spiral)

For Rhiannon

Printed and bound in Great Britain by Page Bros., Norwich

Contents

Preface

The aim of this book is to help experienced and novice teachers improve their
lesson planning. It is not possible, or even desirable in such a short space, to
provide a simple formula or recipe for success that can be applied in all
teaching situations. Instead the book draws on some general principles that
have been highlighted by researchers as having a positive effect on practice.
The result, I hope, is a book which should inform and affect your thinking as
you set about the creative task of preparing and planning your lessons.

Introduction

Teachers as Designers

Planning, it would appear, is central to our existence; we plan meals, holidays, houses, even our families. In short, masses of people express confidence in their ability to control and influence events through the power of forward thinking. Professionals operating in a variety of occupations are no exception: no business manager, for instance, would consider operating in the market-place without some form of corporate plan while no engineer would consider a construction job without detailed plans.

In this sense teachers are very similar. For them planning is a vital activity and is one in which they all engage. A recent report (AMMA, 1991) showed that teachers spent nearly 6 hours a week planning and preparing work compared with almost 17 hours spent teaching in the classroom. Most of this planning, however, is done in private, a process which led Clark and Yinger (1988) to label it as 'the hidden world of teaching'. Within this secret and private world a great deal of the school curriculum is understood, developed and acted upon. Calderhead (1984) has summed it up thus: 'It is in planning that teachers translate syllabus guidelines, institutional expectations and their own beliefs and ideologies of education into guidelines for action in the classroom' (p. 60).

Planning and the nature of professional knowledge

A great deal of teachers' lives is spent in thinking; they think about courses,

1

resources, pupils, as well as how to manage their classes. They also assess their pupils' performance and offer advice and help at every opportunity. The list is endless. A great deal of their time is therefore spent trying to organize and make sense of a welter of competing issues that confront them.

Planning plays a central role in this process. As an activity it is cognitive and behavioural while at the same time highly practical. At one level it means the teacher having to engage in eidetic thinking - visualizing future events - and constructing a map or framework that will guide the action decided upon. At another level it is intensely creative with the teacher devising original solutions to the solving of new and persistent problems. Here Christopher Clark (1989) has claimed the practice of teaching is as 'complex and cognitively demanding as the practice of medicine, law or architecture' (p. 312).

Professional knowledge theorists have claimed that each profession is bound by a set of common mutual operations, what Schon (1984) has called 'design actions'. These are activities predicated to bring about particular desired outcomes in specific contexts. Schon further depicts this process as a 'reflective conversation', where designers enter into a dialogue with the problem and through this dialectical process find a workable solution. Using the above definition, Clark and Peterson (1986) argue that because teachers engage in designing particular courses of action with a view to solving problems that professionalism is inherent in their work. Lesson planning is an essential part of this process.

The image of the teacher that emerges from this conception is of a highly skilled professional who has to orchestrate, manage and solve particular contextual problems. Planning for teachers therefore involves the continuing interaction of several practical and professional procedures for attaining particular ends. In this sense it is a rational process characterized by an attempt to gear teaching to the learning of pupils.

In order to understand the role of planning in teaching it is useful to focus on the three broad domains of teacher operations that seem to frame their work. These are: the pre-active, the inter-active (Jackson, 1968) and the post-active phases (Clark and Peterson, 1986). These distinctions can, however, be misleading because there is no firm line which demarks the ending of one and the beginning of another. Teacher thinking and professional knowledge is more messy than these domains would have us believe. As Clark (1989) again points out, 'the iterative and social nature of teaching allows and encourages revision, postponement, elaboration or abandonment of yesterday's plan in response to today's experiences in the classroom'. Nevertheless, although arbitrary, the distinctions do provide a useful conceptual tool for defining the boundaries of teaching and can be particularly useful when exploring the nature of teachers' planning.

Teachers' plans have also been described in a number of ways - Scripts (Schank and Abelson, 1977), Agendas (Leinhardt and Greeno, 1986), Action Units (Van Parraren, 1979). Whatever the term, it is clear that when constructing them, the teacher draws on a range of experiences and knowledge in an attempt to fit the anticipated and observed needs of a particular lesson or series of lessons.

To understand planning is to understand how teachers transform and interpret knowledge, formulate intentions, and act from that knowledge and those intentions (Clark, 1989). As the National Curriculum approaches, both new and experienced teachers will be faced with new planning challenges. The store of plans in the experienced practitioner's mental bank may have to be replenished and re-edited, whereas the beginner's store will have to be stocked using the new prescriptions as a guide. This book aims to help both groups by examining and presenting new ideas based on current research and theory.

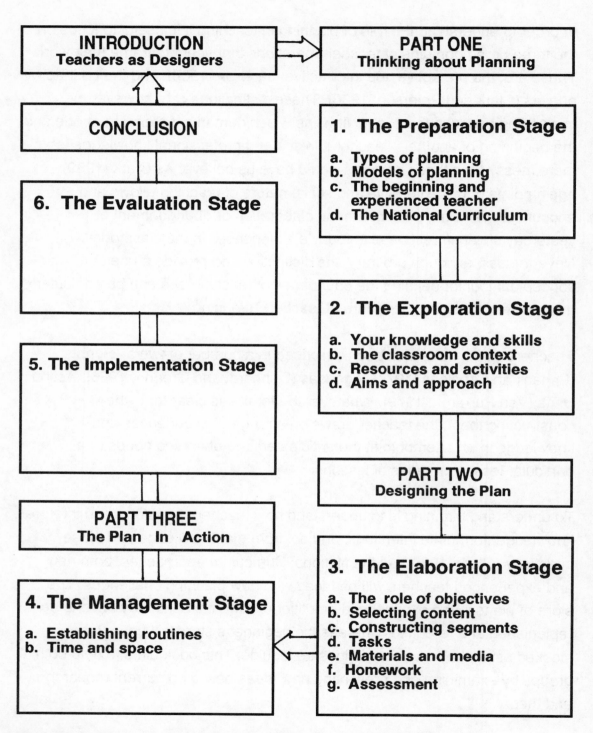

Figure 1: The conceptual structure of the book

Part One

Thinking about Planning

Chapter 1

The Preparation Stage

A great deal of the research into teacher planning has been driven by a desire to understand the complexities of teacher thinking and the ways in which that thinking relates to particular teaching outcomes. This chapter will examine some of these studies and draw out the practical implications for teachers in relation to four particular areas: the types of planning in which teachers engage; the curriculum map and the scheme of work; the models of planning that have been posited and uncovered; and the effect of the National Curriculum on teachers' planning.

Types of planning

Robert Yinger (1977) in a study of elementary school teachers' planning identified a variety of planning activities that typified teaching. These involved the following: daily, weekly, termly, unit and yearly. Roughly translated, the yearly plan would link to the school or department's overall curriculum map which would be tied to the National Curriculum. The termly plan would consist of some aspects of the programmes of study as laid down by the National Curriculum. The unit plan would equate to the 'scheme of work' which links the long-term curriculum map to the more functional daily lesson plan. These unit plans are usually the product of collaborative thinking between colleagues.

Clark and Yinger (1979) in a further examination of the kinds of teacher planning found that there were two broad categories - incremental and comprehensive. The former involved very little advance thought about the wider learning and curricular implications. Here the teachers seemed more intent on trying out ideas or moving quickly on to the next topic. Comprehensive planners, on the other hand, thought more carefully about the whole process and had a longer-term vision of what planning and teaching involved. Their lessons could be placed within the unit or scheme of work and they exhibited clearer ideas in relation to what they wanted to achieve in the classroom.

The curriculum map and scheme of work

The curriculum map and scheme of work have received considerable attention in all the National Curriculum documents and in the more recent specialized HMI Reports. In its broadest sense, the scheme of work is a block of knowledge, skills and understanding which the teacher wishes to develop over the medium term. They are essentially informed by policy statements emanating from school and national level and should indicate clearly how the school and the appropriate department or faculty intends to operationalize these factors. Clearly, these schemes of work must now be related in a logical way to the National Curriculum Programmes of Study and should be a synthesis of the statements of attainment, the content, the teaching strategies and the assessment procedures to be used (Figure 2).

It is usually the responsibility of schools to make provision for the drawing up of these curriculum plans. In addition, given their status, they should be drawn up collaboratively where groups of teachers take responsibility for various aspects of the final document. The final product then forms a bank of information and guidance from which individual or short-term planning can take place. On a wider front they also provide governors, parents, pupils and staff with a careful summary of the departments' and schools' curriculum coverage.

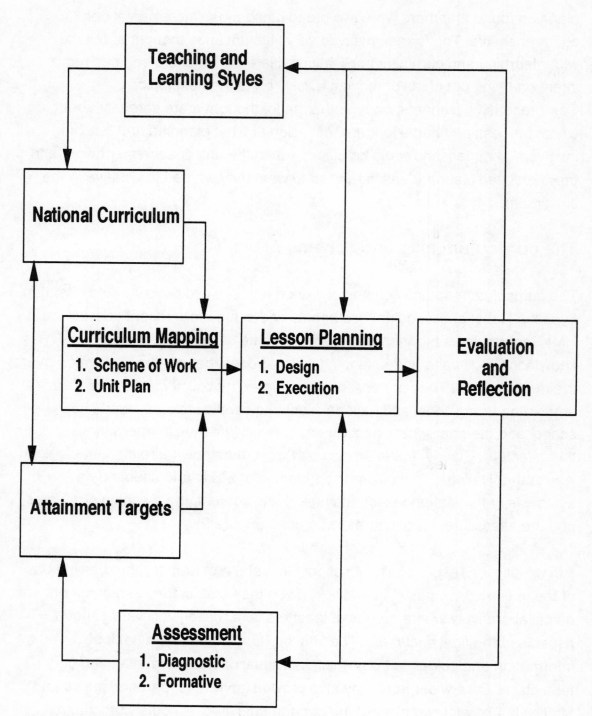

Figure 2: The planning sequence

Schools and individuals can choose a variety of formats for schemes of work, but above all, they should be accessible and flexible. The National Curriculum demands that such planning covers a whole Key Stage so that progression can be coherently planned. However, it is probably more manageable to plan parts of the Key Stage according to years or year groups and then combine the units. These schemes should not be written in tablets of stone but should be sensitive to the changing needs of the school, the pupils and the curriculum.

At secondary level the predominant approach will be through the subject, although in many faculties it will be necessary to indicate the cross-curricular nature of the units. At primary level the whole process will probably be organized around particular domains with each separate subject being addressed through topics or themes.

What key areas should be indicated on a scheme of work?

* **An outline of the essential learning experiences:** this includes the necessary knowledge, understandings and skills inherent in each subject or domain. These will inevitably have cross-curricular implications.

* **The organization and management of the teaching and learning:** this would include outlines of the topics to be covered; the range of teaching styles to be used; the ways of grouping and organizing classes for particular approaches and topics; assessment issues and methods; resource implications and time allocations.

* **Continuity and progression:** here breadth, balance and coverage should relate to the overall structure of the Key Stage.

* **Modes of assessment and evaluation:** these should be linked to the

sorts of teaching and learning methods, the Attainment Targets and the experiences of the pupils.

When planning a unit or scheme of work the following steps may prove useful:

Step 1
Select the topic; ideally this will be done collectively and be part of the decisions based on the National Curriculum programmes of study.

Step 2
Discuss the long-term objectives based on the Attainment Targets. Be sure that there is a careful blend of knowledge, skills, understanding, attitudes, abilities, ideals and appreciations.

Step 3
Prepare an outline of the content coverage if desired. This can be particularly useful for non-specialists working in your department / faculty / area, etc.

Step 4
Plan the types of learning activities to be used:
>   a. Select the teacher-pupil activities and subject matter by which pupils will learn appropriate knowledge skills and abilities.
>   b. Select optional activities based on differentiation.

Step 5
Break the scheme down into manageable individual chunks which will form the basis of the lesson plans during the teaching of the unit.

Step 6
Plan, prepare and secure all the necessary materials and resources for the activities.

Step 7

Plan and prepare the necessary assessment and evaluation materials and exercises.

The relationship between long-range planning epitomized by the scheme of work and the micro-planning characterized by the daily lesson planning is an important one and is the umbilical link which drives the process of teaching and learning. The following diagrams try to conceptualize that link and may help you see the importance of both long-range and short-term planning. The first (Figure 3) illustrates the link between the scheme and everyday teacher planning. The second (Figure 4a and b) gives further examples of unit plans.

Models of planning

The dominant model of lesson planning is that associated with the rational-linear framework begun by Tyler (1950) and further elaborated on by Taba (1956), Popham and Baker (1970) and direct instructional theorists like Gagne and Briggs (1983). This perspective has dominated curriculum texts, teacher preparation programmes and central planning criteria, in spite of contrary research evidence which shows teachers plan in a way which contrasts markedly with the linear process. The model has four basic tenets:

Specifying objectives;

Specifying knowledge and skills;

Selecting and sequencing learning activities;

Evaluating the outcomes.

The model assumes a close link between ends and means; it also assumes that the learning environments in which teaching takes place are static and controllable rather than dynamic. This technical view of planning and teaching, usually stated through the careful specification of detailed behavioural objectives, is designed to promote efficient learning and measurable outcomes.

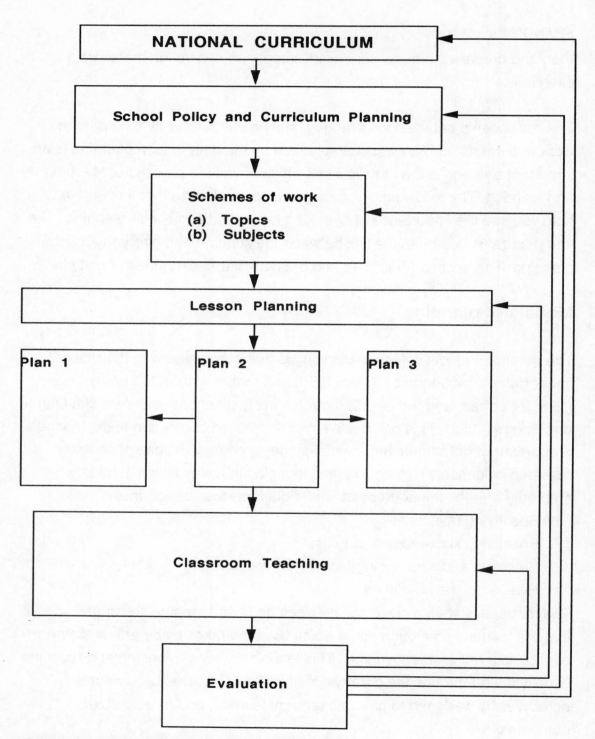

Figure 3: Planning and the curriculum

An alternative model has emerged during the last 15 years. Critics of the rational model (Egan, 1988,1989; Stenhouse, 1975) claim that there is a mismatch between the complexity of classrooms and the specific goals laid out in the plan. They claim that classrooms and lessons have a multiplicity of goals and much of the learning that goes on in them is neither controllable nor predictable in any scientific way. Weick (1979), a fierce critic of the model, claimed the following:

> Organizational actions at best seem to be goal interpreted. Goals are sufficiently diverse, the future is sufficiently uncertain, and the actions on which goal statements should centre are sufficiently unclear that goal statements explain a relatively small portion of the variance in action. It is probable that goals are tied more closely to actual activities than is commonly recognized and that they are more productively understood as summaries of previous actions.

Such critics argue for a non-linear model of planning where teachers start with the activities which in turn produce outcomes (some foreseen, some not) and finally explain their actions by assigning goals to them. Such a theory has been strongly suggested by a number of research studies which have investigated teachers' planning practices. Zahorik (1970, 1975) and Taylor (1970) found that teachers gave the content of lessons and the teaching and learning activities embedded in them a much higher priority in their planning than the delineation of objectives. In fact these aims and objectives seemed to be the least mentioned of all their planning actions. Zahorik also found significant differences between the teachers who planned in detail with objectives and those who did not. The latter it seemed were more responsive to children's needs while the former appeared to pursue their own goals often at the expense of their pupils.

Studies by Joyce and Hartootunian (1964) and Peterson, Marx and Clark

(1978), Sardo-Brown (1990) and John (1991) further indicated the limited adherence to the rational-linear model with teachers preferring to concentrate on the content and the activities designed to bring about learning.

This more organic model of planning and teaching sees objectives in a different way. They are viewed as flowing from a cyclical process and are seen as symbols, advertisements and, in many situations, justifications for action. Although such a descriptive model accounts for a great deal of experienced teachers' planning this does not mean that objectives do not play a highly significant part in the planning and teaching process. Indeed as McLoed (1981) has pointed out, objectives and goals are often embedded in the actions and have become so routinized that they tend not to be explicitly stated, but are nevertheless used.

The question that arises out of these studies is as follows: If objectives-based planning is not used extensively by teachers should the model be abandoned? Apparently not. Zahorik (1970) concluded in his study that the elimination of some form of rational planning would bring about 'random and unproductive learning'. If a lesson is to be effective, it would seem that some direction in the form of goals and experiences, no matter how general or vague, is needed. Instead objectives need to be re-situated and linked far more closely to context-bound considerations. Seeing the potential in a situation may lead to more achievable goals, and embedding goals more deeply in the teacher's personal-professional knowledge may have a more beneficial effect.

Too often, goals or objectives are seen and used as remote, cold, technical instruments which have to be laid out in a specific way often to satisfy external agencies. It is this artificial use of objectives that is potentially damaging.

The National Curriculum

The advent of the National Curriculum has meant that the task of long-term and short-term planning has become far more meaningful in recent years. Teachers in all of the Key Stages have spent an enormous amount of time and energy in coming to terms with the welter of new statutory requirements and orders which have emanated from the National Curriculum Council and other bodies. As this book is being constructed most primary and secondary schools will be teaching the programmatic requirements associated with six of the nine National Curriculum areas.

The framework provided by the new curriculum means that planning now involves not only the mapping out of the essential knowledge and skills of particular subjects but also the laying down of the course objectives, the teaching and learning styles to be used and the sorts of assessment strategies that will have to be deployed. At primary level this often means reconciling the subject requirements with a long-standing commitment to integrated topic work. Thus when preparing to teach, full use will have to be made of the National Curriculum programmes of study. Schemes of work must include references to the Attainment Targets and the sorts of tasks that may bring about the long- and short-term achievement of those targets.

The problem here may be to do with translation. Fundamental to this process is the notion of uniqueness; the National Curriculum may be the framework within which teachers operate but as professionals, planning simply for the National Curriculum alone can never be anything other than barren. For planning lessons is a dynamic process affected by many types and intensities of endogenous and exogenous forces. Thus it is important to think of the National Curriculum as a framework within which lesson plans will be crafted.

However, the National Curriculum can help teachers' planning by providing answers to two important questions:

* Which are the most noteworthy things that happen in a classroom?
* How can I plan so that I can address these salient events?

Here the Attainment Targets and statements of attainment provide useful scaffolding for the preparation of lessons and the emergence of strategies that effectively address the above questions. These statements can help focus the mind of the teacher on the important classroom events and give coherence to plans in relation to children's learning (SEAC, 1990).

UNIT PLANNING SHEET		
UNIT: NC (AT / Level): CLASS:	Time available: Class HW	Pre-requisites:

Concepts / Language	Content Analysis (Topic Web, Flow chart?)	Teaching styles / Strategies
Potential difficulties? Research, Teaching		Starting points
Homework		Resources to support teaching (software, video, text)
Assessment / Evaluation		Applications
What does it lead on to?		Cross curricular links

Figure 4a: Unit planning sheet

Adapted with permission of the mathematics PGCE group, University of Bristol

	PLANNING GRID FOR STUDY UNITS IN KEY STAGES 2 AND 3							
Year : Title :	Study Unit :			Focus :				
	Key Issues	Concepts	Content	Resources, Types of Sources	Activities	Teaching and Learning Methods	ATs	Links with Other Subjects

Figure 4b: Planning grid

Multiple copies may be made by the purchaser © Peter D. John 1993

Chapter 2

The Exploration Stage

Introduction

The previous chapter reviewed some of the research that has been carried out on teacher planning and offered advice on macro-planning. This chapter will explore the intermediate stage of the preparation process as it relates to the planning of specific lessons and is therefore more concerned with what might be termed micro-planning. This phase has four key interrelated elements and will explore the nature of the teacher's knowledge and skills, the classroom context, resources for learning, and the importance of approaches and strategies.

Appraising your knowledge and skills

Smith (1985) has commented that one of the strongest influences on teachers' curriculum planning was their perception of the subject matter, the types of knowledge it represented and the methods and activities appropriate to teach it. Borko et al. (1988) further claimed that teachers' patterns of planning were clearly related to their subject matter specializations. Taylor (1975) and Peterson, Marx and Clark (1978) similarly found that when planning, teachers often started with the content to be taught rather than with the objectives to be achieved.

In recent years there has been considerable research into teachers' knowledge of the content and the way their understanding effects planning, teaching and learning (Shulman 1986; Shulman and Sykes, 1987; Grossman, 1987; Hasweh, 1987; Wilson, Shulman and Richert, 1988). HMI have similarly pointed to the close relationship that exists between the teacher's own knowledge and understanding and the quality of his/her teaching. Clearly successful teaching depends on the curricular expertise and professional craft knowledge of the teacher but an essential element of this knowledge and expertise relates to the teacher's own understanding of the subject matter to be taught (Wilson and Wineburg, 1988; McDermaid et al., 1989; DES, 1992; Carre and Bennett, 1992; John, 1992).

At this stage in the planning process, checking personal knowledge and understanding of the material to be taught, in relation to the programmes of study as laid down by the National Curriculum would seem a sensible starting point. Research has shown that this is particularly important for beginning teachers who often lack the curricular expertise of their more experienced counterparts. In fact investigations into beginning teachers' planning reveals that one of the first steps they take is to appraise and assess their knowledge of the topic to be taught (Broekmanns, 1986; John, 1992).

So, when thinking about the lesson, it would make sense to simultaneously consider the subject matter to be taught. This advice can be operationalized in three ways: the **first** is to consider the content as valuable in itself, thus to know it is intrinsically good and useful. The **second**, is to think of the content as having a utilitarian value in that it can be useful either vocationally, socially or for leisure . The **third**, is to think of the subject matter as a vehicle for the teaching and development of various skills, processes and abilities.

However, it must be remembered that the process of translating the store of old and newly acquired subject matter, knowledge and skills into plans for classroom use is not a straightforward process (Calderhead, 1988). Indeed, planning relies heavily on the interrelationship between various forms of knowledge and skill that gradually shapes the content into worthwhile learning experiences for pupils.

The classroom context

The architect cannot design a building without reference to its environment. He/she has to take into account a number of factors that have nothing to do with the purpose for which the building is designed. He/she may for example, have to give up his/her intention of giving the building a particular shape; the design may have to be modified in respect of the materials available. In the end the finished product will be an amalgam of compromises within the constraints of time, money, environment and expertise. The teacher is similarly situated. He/she cannot plan entirely in a vacuum. The lesson has to relate to the many conditions outside the immediate control of the practitioner. These conditions constitute the context of teaching.

In the introductory chapter teaching was presented as a problem-solving process. In this sense teachers are faced with a number of variables that influence the planning decisions they have to take. Research has shown that teachers often begin the process of planning with reference to this working environment and from that, their thinking fans out to include learning objectives, resources, methods and approaches. Teachers' planning, therefore, takes place against this backcloth of concerns and constraints which in turn influences the selection of learning activities more than the rational model suggests (Kyriacou, 1984).

The beginning teacher, however, not only lacks detailed contextual knowledge but also lacks the experience upon which to make informed judgements. Take a car mechanic, for instance, who when learning his/her trade is forced to follow step-by-step rules for fault diagnosis. However, as the mechanic develops a store of information he/she forms various conceptual models of certain car types and begins to associate particular faults with particular models of car. Once these heuristics have been sufficiently internalized, the mechanic can often spot faults and develop a quick diagnosis without having to follow the traditional route.

An important element in learning about planning is, therefore, the intelligent utilization of professional knowledge. The development of such expert knowledge takes time and the beginning teacher, in particular, needs to think carefully about every aspect of the teaching context before embarking on lesson preparation. Two distinct questions therefore arise out of this issue: Firstly, what sort of contextual knowledge is most useful and worthwhile for teachers during this exploratory phase of planning? Secondly, how can this information be obtained, gathered and utilized effectively?

Below are some guidelines that may help answer those very questions.

Specific information needed about the specific classes to be taught

* **Age:** Ascertain the precise range of ages in the class.

* **Ability:** Find out what range of ability exists in the class. This will obviously link to the curriculum and educational policy of the school. For instance, are groups set, banded, streamed, mixed ability? How many children with learning difficulties are there in the class? What sort of support is available for them?

* **Composition and chemistry:** What is the gender split? Are there

children from ethnic groups? What are their needs? How well do the group gell? Are there any personal feuds and difficult personalities?

* **Motivation:** What level of motivation can be expected? What sort of routines are they used to? What teaching and learning styles best motivate the group? How long is their concentration span?

* **Behaviour:** What sort of behaviour can be expected? What sort of teacher approach do they best respond to? Are there any pupils with specific behavioural problems? If so, how can they best be handled? What sort of disciplinary approach should be used?

* **Size and layout:** How many pupils are there in the group? How is the class usually laid out and why? If they work in groups how are they constructed - ability, friendship, gender balance etc.? How might they react to a change of seating?

* **Previous work:** What do the pupils know and understand about the topics to be taught? What previous work have they completed? How have they reacted to the topic(s) so far? What is their level of interest and understanding?

* **Equipment:** Will special equipment be needed? What is available? Can it be booked? Are there any safety precautions? What effect will the practical elements have on the lesson?

* **Timing:** At what time of the day is the lesson due to take place? What lesson precedes and follows it?

How and where to find that information

* Observations: These are central to planning particularly in the early stages and are the raw material for much of beginning teachers' contextual knowledge. Ensure observations are systematic, regular and well recorded. To clarify your observations discuss what you have seen and recorded with the teacher. But remember, do not be judgemental! Questions should be for further clarification only.

* Talk to colleagues: Your colleagues are a mine of information about their classes. Accessing that knowledge is a skilful process and should be done formally and informally as the opportunity arises.

* Heads of department/subject co-ordinators: These are among the most important and knowledgeable people in any school. They can help by giving you information about the departmental structure, its ethos, the most popular and effective teaching approaches used, the sorts of resources and support available, etc. They will also have syllabuses, schemes of work and assessment procedures.

* Year/pastoral tutor: These carry useful pastoral information about relevant individual pupils and should be consulted at every opportunity.

Resources and activities

Research into experienced teachers' planning has shown that the search for activities in relation to resources is high on the list of teachers' planning priorities. Taylor (1970) discovered that one of their first planning tasks was to address factors associated with the teaching context, particularly the construction of resources and materials which were linked to pupils' interests. Zahorik (1975) similarly found that the development of classroom tasks were among experienced teachers' main concerns. Research on novice teachers' planning found similar but more marked tendencies to identify early on the sorts of activities and resources around which lessons could be built (Broekmanns, 1986; John, 1991). Overall, it seems that the search for appropriate materials and ideas for possible activities is carried out for a number of reasons:

a. To glean ideas about possible approaches.

b. To gain further information about the topic of the lesson.

c. To see how other teachers and text books approached the topic.

d. To help build a mental picture of how the lesson(s) may run.

Thus during this exploratory phase of planning the search for activities and resources ranks high in teachers' thoughts. Below is a list of ideas concerning the location and use of resources which may be of help in this stage of your preparation.

Location

* Diagram of location (Figure 5).

* Student teachers should familiarize themselves fully with the method or curriculum area in their training institution. They should also investigate their placement or partner school's resource area and subject department. It is important to remember to check the booking systems for equipment, particularly specialist equipment in science, etc. Be careful to ask about the limitations on the use of particular resources in terms of cost and usability.

* The local teachers' centre is important and regular visits will prove most worthwhile. They will have information about the wider use and location of resources.

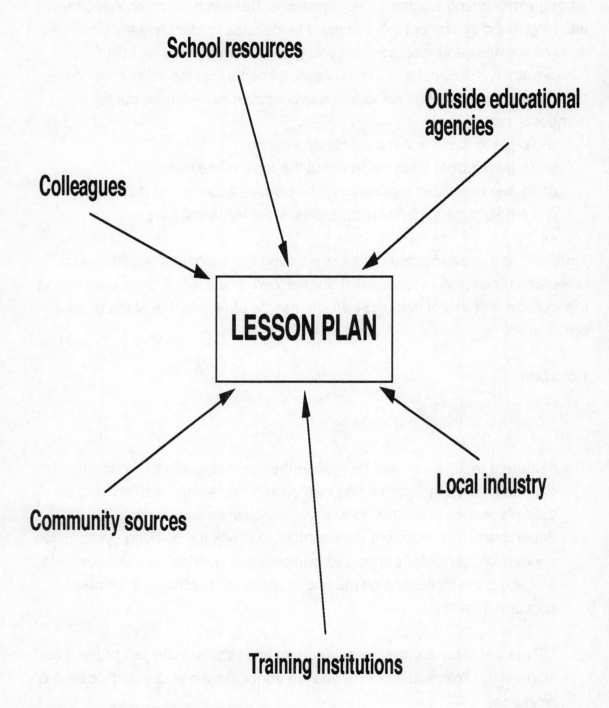

Figure 5: Resource locations

* The local museum education service is very useful. They have a range of services in all subject areas and can be a source of inspiration and ideas for lessons.

* Libraries need to be checked both in school and in the locality for resources and borrowing facilities.

* Ensure you contact the information technology co-ordinator and acquaint youself with the procedures associated with the use of the micro-computer network.

* The school's industrial liaison officer/community co-ordinator can be useful in getting speakers and other resources.

Method and approach

Method is a blanket term used to describe the sorts of strategies and techniques used to bring about learning. These methods concern the way teachers organize and use techniques, subject matter, teaching tools, materials and tasks to meet their objectives. Selecting teaching strategies is, therefore, bound up with other important determinants of planning and teaching.

These strategies are then operationally defined. Despite fashions and accepted notions of good practice, there is still no clearly defined accepted best practice. Instead there are a host of competing strategies all of which can be effective and useful to the teacher. This eclectic mix must be tailored for the purpose to which it is going to be put. Remember two teaching situations are never identical and your approach must be flexible enough to adapt to changing circumstances.

Of prime importance during this stage of your planning is the need to think about the type of lesson you envisage giving and the sort of teaching strategies you intend to use. These thoughts will be inextricably linked to the learning outcomes you are hoping to achieve. However, at this stage these ideas need not be definite; instead it may be better to have some broad notion of the sort of lesson you hope to give and what you would like to achieve in terms of learning. This image will in some way be tied to your knowledge of the class and how previous lessons have run. Firming up these methodological ideas and broad learning aims will occur when you have had time to internalize and evaluate your teaching.

From this vantage point, both theoretically and practically, there are no obvious advantages to be gained from starting with too clearly defined objectives; it is not mandatory and research has shown that it is not even practical. Very often it is best to begin where you feel most comfortable. Try not to impose rigid objectives too early on in your preparation. They are useful, as we will see in the next chapter, but they must not make your planning inflexible and hidebound. At this stage you may well have a multiplicity of goals for your particular lesson(s) but these are likely to be approximations and it is probably better to recycle these as your notion of how the lesson may run becomes clearer. Tuning your methodological or strategic approaches and general aims into your various contextual and resource wavelengths is perhaps a more powerful way of clarifying your goals and objectives for the next more formal planning stage.

Part Two

Designing the Plan

Chapter 3

The Elaboration Stage

Introduction

This section will be concerned with the issue of plan construction. As has been pointed out, the routine or daily lesson plan is the key document in the process of teaching. Essentially, it is a script which is prepared in advance and acts as the guide for a particular lesson. Just as no professional can ever be successful without a clear plan of operation, so a teacher who continually improvises eventually produces inaccurate learning.

The role of objectives

Kyriacou (1991) outlined four essential ingredients of a successful lesson plan:

    a. The delineation of objectives.
    b. The selecting and scripting of the lesson.
    c. The preparation of the props to be used.
    d. Deciding on the best method for assessing pupils' learning.

Virtually all major guide books on curriculum and lesson planning begin with the importance of laying down at an early stage the educational and learning goals that will guide the lesson. The role of objectives has, therefore, become sacrosanct in all the major books and manuals dealing with the planning of teaching and learning. Basically the concept rests on the notion, that if you do not know where you are going from the outset, then not only are you likely to get lost on the way, but you may not even know when you have arrived.

The arguments for and against the use of objectives in planning have received some attention from theorists and researchers (see Ormell, 1992 for a full and up-to-date review). MacDonald-Ross (1973) in a discussion of the pros and cons of objectives in planning and teaching concluded his discussion with the following summary:

Advantages:

* They form the basis for a well-worked-out method of rational planning.

* They encourage teachers to think and plan in detailed specific terms.

* They provide a rational basis for evaluation and assessment of action and learning.

* They help the teacher construct appropriate teaching strategies.

Disadvantages:

* Defining objectives too closely at the outset of planning makes the process of planning rigid.

* Laying down objectives too closely can inhibit opportunist learning.

* Objectives do not help teachers deal with unpredicted classroom events.

* There are an infinite number of pathways through a particular topic and strict adherence to objectives reduces the effectiveness of the design.

* Learning opportunities often emerge during lessons and prescription too early on may blind the teacher.

* Objectives are inherently ambiguous and the level of specificity is often problematic.

* Trivial and over-simplified objectives, which are often the easiest to operationalize, may be used too frequently.

Research evidence seems to show that there is a mismatch between this theoretical framework and the reality of classroom teaching. Teachers, it appears, from nearly all the studies carried out, do not always start with objectives, preferring instead to be flexible. Often they start with activities, the context, the content and the tasks being set (Taylor, 1975; Zahorik, 1970; Clark and Yinger, 1988; Sardo-Brown, 1990; John, 1991). Objectives are often hidden in the planning process and occur at various points within it.

This clearly poses a problem for the beginning teacher. Experienced teachers it seems, have well-developed routines and procedures as well as a store of professional knowledge which includes information and images of how typical lessons will run. Their planning is, therefore, of a different character to that of their less experienced counterparts. Beginning teachers have to rely on more advanced, detailed and staged planning to be successful in the classroom. Gaea Leinhardt (1989) conducted a comparative study of the planning skills of experienced and inexperienced maths teachers. She found that those with longer service had better developed and more complete mental note-pads and agendas for teaching. They also built in and used checkpoints to monitor that pupils were learning and understanding the lesson. Thus according to Leinhardt:

Experienced teachers weave a series of lessons together to form an instructional topic in a way that consistently builds upon and advances materials introduced in prior lessons. Experts also construct lessons that display a highly efficient within lesson structure, one that is characterized by fluid movement from one type of activity to another . . . novice teachers' lessons on the other hand, are characterized by fragmented lesson structures with long transitions between lesson segments . . . Their lessons do not fit well together within or across topic boundaries.

Objectives for both the novice and veteran teacher should, therefore, be approached flexibly as they can vary from the very complex to the simple and straightforward. A variety of guides and taxonomies have been produced to help teachers formulate and choose appropriate objectives. These have now been supplemented by the National Curriculum Attainment Targets which lay down a staged process of assessment. However, during the process of planning, the teacher must use his/her professional judgement concerning the relative importance of the Attainment Targets and their relationship to the lesson objectives. To help you in this process, some examples of different types of learning objectives and the criteria for their selection are listed below.

Behavioural objectives

These are based on the notion that for teaching goals to be meaningful they must be clearly communicated and should relate to what the pupil will be doing and the standard of performance required of him / her. Thus most behavioural objectives start with precise propellent verbs, for instance, write, list, identify, classify, compare, analyse, etc. Such statements have become accepted in recent years because they are clearly defined and unambiguous.

Critics have claimed that such a process is reductionist and leads to the neglect of other important affective and cognitive areas of growth. Thus teachers who home in on specifics could run the risk of neglecting the wider elements of learning or perhaps ignoring other important objectives because of an overreliance on the manageable aspects of behaviour. In addition, critics have pointed out that many important cognitive processes, for instance, problem solving in mathematics, is not readily observable or measurable in a behavioural sense.

Generic objectives

As an antidote to the specificity of behavioural objectives, curriculum theorists have advocated the incorporation of more affective elements into the construction and choice of objectives. Thus the words understand, appreciate, value and explore have been used to complement the more rigid behaviourist approach. In this way an initial objective or Attainment Target could be broken down at each stage to guide the lesson.

The various taxonomies that have been produced provide a guide to understanding these complexities. Although various weaknesses can be identified in such taxonomies both they and objectives provide teachers with a way of linking their teaching to the learning of their pupils. In this sense they are valuable planning tools particularly for the beginning teacher who is in the process of developing a body of professional knowledge and skills. In relation to the National Curriculum the statements of attainment can help you define and refine your objectives. It may help at this stage of the planning process to identify the broad statements your lesson plan will promote and to build these into your more precise objectives and activities. The following may help you evaluate the use of objectives and statements of attainment in your planning (Figure 6).

Format and components

In some schools particular planning formats are designated. However, given

Take five teaching and learning objectives from a lesson plan related to the National Curriculum and list them below.

	OBJECTIVE	RATING
1		
2		
3		
4		
5		

Rate each either (g) good, (f) fair or (p) poor according to the level achieved during any one lesson. Now think about each objective:
Was there any aspect of the writing of it that hindered its use in the plan?
What was its relationship to the National Curriculum Attainment Targets?
How far did you achieve the objectives?
How could you improve them in the light of experience?

Multiple copies may be made by the purchaser © Peter D. John 1993.

Figure 6: Outlining objectives

the personalized and idiosyncratic nature of planning, sticking to one prototype may be inhibiting. Despite variations each plan does have a fairly well agreed set of components. These may be described differently but consist of the following:

> * A set of objectives, goals or targets. These can vary in precision depending on what is being studied and the personal characteristics of the teacher and class.

* The materials/resources needed for the lesson. This could range from specialist equipment to simple text books.

* Some reference to the subject matter under study. This may be intertwined with the method but should still be observable and clear.

* The teaching method or approach. Here the teaching tactics should be laid out clearly, sequentially and be related to the subject matter, knowledge and understanding or whatever is the vehicle for the strategy.

* The tasks and activities.

* The timing of the phases of the lesson.

* An evaluation of the lesson.

Clearly formats come in all shapes and sizes. On the following pages are some examples of such models. Some of them are generic in that they can apply to any lesson type, while some are examples of formats for particular lessons.

Selecting content

An important area of planning is the decision made about the content of the lesson. Each lesson or learning activity should have at its core some subject matter knowledge. The desired outcomes in relation to that knowledge may vary but the content still forms the vehicle for a great many of the tasks and activities that teachers set.

The selection of the appropriate content is a complex and sophisticated skill. The key areas are the parameters of the content and the depth of knowledge

FORMAT 1

Lesson Topic :
Group :

Date :
Time / Period :

Aims / Objectives

Content

Procedure

Resources / Materials

Evaluation

FORMAT 2

Lesson Topic : Group :	Date : Time / Period :
Objectives	
Procedure	**Content**
Evaluation	
Tasks **Homework** **Resources**	

FORMAT 3

| Lesson Topic : | | Date : |
| Group : | | Time / Period : |

Objectives / Goals	Time	Activities / Strategies
1.		1.
2.		2.
3.		3.
4.		4.
5.		5.

Resources

Tasks

Evaluation

FORMAT 4		
Lesson Topic :		Date :
Group :		Period / Time :

Aims / Objectives	
Knowledge and Understanding	
Skills and Abilities	
Attitudes	

Time	Method	Materials / Resources

Evaluation

FORMAT 5 - for Group Work Lesson		
Lesson Topic : Group :		Date : Period / Time :
Objectives		
Resources		
Organization		
	Group 1 Activities	Group 2 Activities	Group 3 Activities
Homework Evaluation		

Multiple copies may be made by the purchaser © Peter D. John 1993.

FORMAT 6 - for more direct teaching

Lesson Topic : Group:	Date : Time / Period :

Knowledge and Understanding to be developed

Objectives / Targets

Time	**Phase and Activities**	**Resources**
—		
—		
—		
—		
—		
—		
—		
—		

Pitfalls to avoid **During teaching**	**Transitions**	**Ending**

Evaluation

FORMAT 7 - Problem Solving Lesson

Lesson Topic :
       Group:

       Date :
       Time / Period :

Objectives / Goals

Resources

Problems to be solved

Time	Phase and Activities	Resources
—		
—		
—		
—		
—		
—		
—		
—		

Evaluation

required to achieve the particular purposes of the lesson. Such decisions are crucial and interact with the problem of task setting, resource choice and construction and the teaching strategy adopted. The selection process will also to some extent influence the desired learning outcomes. Here, once again, the differences between the beginning and experienced teacher become quite marked.

For the novice, equipping themselves with the right level of knowledge can be a difficult process. Many new teachers often overload themselves with content and risk planning and teaching lessons as simply the delivery of inert knowledge. On the other hand, having the knowledge can and does provide the new teacher with the necessary confidence when facing classes for the first time. Getting the balance right and seeing the learning potential in the content is a difficult process. For experienced teachers, the problem is often one of keeping abreast of new developments and ensuring their understanding is complete. This has gained in importance with the emergence of the National Curriculum.

For the teacher the choice of subject matter is also linked to its transformative quality; in other words, how can the knowledge be transformed to be of use in the lesson so that the pupils can learn. Thus teachers have to psychologize the subject matter so that it can be utilized in the classroom (Dewey, 1902).

With the advent of the National Curriculum, content has taken on new importance. Teachers have to ensure that there is a congruence between the subject matter coverage and the assessment structure. The development and deployment of Standard Assessment Tests, both mandatory and non-mandatory, will in many ways guide the coverage of content. However, research from the USA has shown that despite central prescriptions, too often teachers failed to cover the content adequately and in sufficient depth and breadth so that children had a base from which to complete assessment tasks.

Thus the process of familiarization with the content areas of the National Curriculum is a vital first step for both beginning and experienced teachers. For primary school teachers this is perhaps even more imperative given the wide range of knowledge required by each subject area (McNamara, 1990; John, 1992).

Here particular criteria can help guide the selection and organization of the content:

Validity: The content selected from the National Curriculum should be verifiable, not misleading.

Significance: The salient areas of the subject topic should be chosen to avoid cluttering the lesson with insignificant content.

Balance: Pupils should have access to macro-and micro-knowledge; both the sweep and depth in each topic area.

Interest: Try to ensure that the content is interesting to help foster successful learning.

Utility: Choose content according to its usefulness for future learning both inside and outside the classroom.

Accessibility: Make sure the content chosen is well within the range of the abilities in your class.

Feasibility: Ensure your choice is feasible given the demands of the National and school curriculum. Always remember there are limitations.

Constructing segments

When preparing your plan it is vital that each segment of the lesson fits into a coherent whole. These intertwined elements are the building blocks of a lesson and the linking of each is a vital ingredient in any planning recipe (Leinhardt, 1989). Each segment should relate to a number of different activities or tasks. These could be teacher led or pupil driven. Take for instance two of the most important sections in any lesson, the opening and closing segments.

The **impact or introductory** segment, as the word implies, seeks to open the lesson and as such can take a variety of forms. It may serve as a simple instruction-giving phase or it may be used to link previous lesson(s) to the present one. Many experienced teachers like to use this section to set the scene for the rest of the lesson whether by laying out the aims of the lesson or by flagging the key points to be covered. It can also be used effectively to motivate the class with a clever or interesting start. Whetting the appetite is an important part of classroom teaching and thinking up such opening gambits is a central part of planning and preparation.

During this introductory phase the teacher should try to plan to:
   a. Arouse maximum interest in the lesson.
   b. Inform the pupils about the lesson and its purpose.
   c. Show the relationship of the lesson to previous ones and flag the next stage.

Whatever the purpose, this introduction should be planned with considerable care; such clarity will help to move the lesson through its more awkward areas.

The **feedback** segment, although appearing at the end of the lesson, can also serve a number of useful functions. It can be the point when the teacher formally checks for understanding or it can be used more profitably for monitoring learning. It can serve as a link between the present and future lessons or, on a more formal level, the teacher could use it to check learning against the explicit objectives laid out at the start.

Whatever strategy is adopted it is important never to assume learning is taking place in class just because some pupils give correct answers to your questions. To ensure you are evaluating the range of knowledge and skills you have planned it is important when preparing to carefully structure your **review** segments. The substance of this feedback could take many forms. Below is a list that may guide you when constructing feedback sessions:

a. Try to pose several thought-provoking questions that summarize the learning areas you have covered in the lesson.
b. Ask for comparisons with what has already been learned in previous lessons.
c. Ask a pupil to summarize the main ideas or areas of the lesson.
d. Have a short quiz.
e. Talk to groups and individuals; ask them evaluative questions during the important stages of the lesson.

In conjunction with this try to have as many medial summaries as possible during the lesson. Here a series of pivotal questions can be asked after covering an important concept, idea or area of knowledge. Such summaries slow down a lesson, bring together information and can be phased in at various levels. They can also be carried out with groups who may be working at differing levels. They are particularly helpful for low ability children who need help in comprehending new information and making links with prior knowledge. Medial summaries should then be linked to the final concluding feedback segment.

The key to effective planning is to ensure that all your segments, whether they include activities or particular tasks are carefully **timed**. This is a difficult exercise for beginning teachers who frequently complain of overrunning activities. Occasionally, this can be cured by going through segments in your mind before inter-active teaching begins; **imaging** a lesson in this way may help to overcome this problem. In doing so use previous successful lessons that have been observed and delivered as mental models to guide your thoughts.

When considering the timing it is important for all teachers to keep the **pace** of the lesson moving according to the ability and sorts of activities that have been set. Some exercises require slow, careful attention, whereas others need speed and accuracy. Always plan to keep up the momentum by avoiding breaks and fragmentation which can lead to boredom or management problems.

Doyle (1983) has estimated that at least 15 per cent of classroom time is spent moving from one activity to another. So when planning your timing try to see yourself as the conductor of an orchestra. Before taking the rostrum the conductor has usually played out each movement and timed its intensity and duration while still allowing for elements of improvisation. During the performance he is then more able to keep the various instruments together, while allowing for the individuality of each. Orchestrating the **transitions** between each section of the lesson is therefore vital to achieve overall smoothness in your teaching. Timing these transitions and integrating them into your planning can only enhance the success of your lessons.

Over twenty years ago, Michael Marland commented that 'a lesson is a presentation, however much pupil participation there is, and its **rhythm and pace** are part of the enjoyment. So when a pupil declares late in the day "that was a good lesson", it is frequently the pacing of the lesson which created the feeling of satisfaction. Lesson plans need shape and it is often the relationship between the segments that creates the rhythm. The variations in the lesson should therefore be carefully planned to give the learning process its **vitality.** The following three points may help you produce that vitality:

* Plan to involve the pupils as much as possible in their own learning. Gaining fresh insights and understanding new knowledge is intrinsically motivating and makes lessons gratifying and worthwhile.

* Ensure your lessons have a variety of activities and are taught using a variety of techniques. Remember one method will never be suitable for all pupils, just as some objectives can never be attained by each student to the same level. However, ensure these changes are built into the rhythm and routine of the classroom; do not make them disruptive but try to build them into the overall structure of the lesson.

* Use as many lively activities as you can. These often inject pace into lessons because they encourage participation.

Tasks

The concept of academic task has been central to much of the research on teaching in the last decade. Tasks have thus been defined as the 'stimuli that help pupils engage in thinking about and demonstrating competence in the content of lessons' (Doyle, 1983).

Doyle (1983) has outlined the generic components of a task and claims it consists of at least four elements: **a product**, for instance a set of questions, statements; a series of **operations** that have to be completed; a set of **resources** which form the context of the task, e.g. a textbook, worksheet, information handout; and an **accountability** or significance system which includes the weight and assessment of the task in relation to its importance. These tasks are embedded into an activity structure which then further defines their purpose and provides the context for their completion.

Seen in this way tasks are the mechanisms by which teachers begin to develop cognitive activity in their pupils according to subject area. The completion of these tasks then provides the teacher with evidence about the extent of the learning that has taken place and information about the efficacy of the task itself. Tasks are therefore selected and constructed for their ability to promote learning in a manner intended by the teacher.

Berieter and Scardamelia (1985) suggest that the reproduction of inert academic knowledge is too often promoted in classroom tasks. Similarly with the arrival of an overcrowded National Curriculum and a more formal set of assessment structures, teachers may well become more concerned with coverage of content rather than the process of learning. Despite this they suggest that during planning teachers can influence the levels of intrinsic motivation and learning by developing more meaningful problem-solving tasks and by applying more positive reward structures.

Finally, Marshall and Weinstein (1985) stress the importance of preparing tasks according to the needs of pupils and ensuring that all questions, statements and exercises are differentiated according to the abilities in the class. There are numerous strategies for achieving this. Below are summaries of some of the most popular approaches:

* Differentiating the **length and degree** of complexity of the task. The key tool here is the tailored activity; in this approach all pupils work on common activities but the work is stepped so that pupils can progress according to their speed and inclination.

* Another approach is to differentiate the **type** of work that your pupils will do. For example, setting various tasks and assigning them according to the skills and abilities of the pupils. The problem with this is that firstly, you have to differentiate openly within the same class and secondly, it requires the production of numerous 'lessons within lessons' which can be complicated and time consuming.

* Grouping within the classroom is becoming more popular and this does have the advantage of allowing the teacher to plan work according to age or ability. Tasks can then be planned and set accordingly. However, this approach can be divisive and makes a mockery of the mixed ability approach which emphasizes collaborative learning.

So when planning tasks, take care to avoid the continual reproduction of inert material which simply requires standard routine answers. Such tasks according to Doyle (1986) and John (1993) make up between one-third and one-half of all classroom activities. Try to ensure that some of your tasks ask for higher order cognitive processes with the focus on interpretation, explanation, analysis, application and the assembly of information from a variety of sources. To help you plan writing tasks it may be useful to use the following framework developed from the Northern Examination Board's Standard Assessments in Literacy.

* Make an early decision about the purpose of the written communication. These aims can be usefully narrowed down into three essential elements: **focus, use** and **organization.** The first construct of **focus** suggests there are three options or directions for the communication: writer, reader or subject. Whatever focus is chosen it is important to take into account the audience which in the case of writing may be large and far removed. The second construct of **use** is associated with purpose. Here it is important to specify the statements they are going to use, expand on these in the course of the task and finally to examine the writing critically. The final **organization** section suggests that the writing be structured in one of three ways: by time, group or theme.

These generic typologies can then be structured into three major categories of writing task: narration, argumentation and exposition.

These genres include some of the following types of writing:

Narration	**Exposition**	**Argumentation**
Personal account	Instruction	Opinion
Imaginative account	Description	Persuasion
Report	Explanation	Argument
Narrative	Information	Analysis
Reflection	Compare/contrast	

This framework may help you plan writing tasks that are more meaningful and relevant in terms of variation and purpose.

Resources

A key aspect of task construction is the production of appropriate resources. The time and attention given to the creation and presentation of various materials and media can often mark the success or failure of lessons. Shulman (1986) has called these teaching aids the 'materia medica' of the teaching profession and claims that the way in which these are developed, thought about and used represents teachers' professional knowledge in action. For pupils these resources are often the lens through which they view the subject.

Kyriacou (1990) has called this process 'prop preparation' and claims that the term refers to all the materials to be called upon in a lesson, for instance, the writing and running of multiple copies of worksheets or the ordering, booking and checking of equipment. The teacher's selection and construction of these materials should be tied closely to the general thrust of the lesson. For example, the readability of a worksheet and the task structure employed should be linked to the broad objectives and the content set out in the plan. In conjunction with this, such resources should be tied to the age and ability range in the class, the time available, the teaching strategy being adopted, the layout of the classroom and the likely reaction of the pupils.

Often such resources can be found and utilized relatively quickly. In Chapter 3 you were given a list of possible resource areas. Check these carefully before deciding on the final format. Remember text books are produced for this very purpose - read them, make a mental note of useful chapters or sections or even pictures and diagrams. Look up the store of departmental or school worksheets/information sheets, etc. Similarly, seek out pre-prepared and published transparencies, documents, work schemes and audio-visual material.

However, when considering these pre-packed resources remember they have often been constructed either for a specific class (usually the case with colleagues' material) or for a wide audience (usually the case with published material). The variation is therefore wide so do not overuse 'off-the-peg' material. It may not fit and adapting the ideas is more time consuming but improves the appropriateness of resources and therefore your chances of success.

When you prepare your own resources use the wide variety of presentational aids available to you. Although the banda is fast, it does not always produce the best finish. Presentation is important and often reflects on your professionalism. Remember pupils often see both you and the subject through the materials that are given to them. Use word processors and desk-top publishing packages whenever possible; these allow you to edit materials and guarantee good quality presentation.

Thus many lessons are less than successful because inadequate and inappropriate resources have been prepared. Your materials and media should therefore be:

    a. Accurate.

    b. Well laid out and readable.

    c. Interesting and varied.

    d. Linked to the objectives and content of the lesson.

    e. Used constructively.

Below is a table of the types of resources you could develop and some suggestions as to how they might be used in your planning.

* *View/observe*	*Read*	*Listen*
Visual	**Materials**	**Media**
Bulletins	Books	Audio
Banners	Comic strip	Tapes
Posters	Pamphlets	Records
Transparencies	Posters	**Verbal**
Slides	Newspapers	Speeches
Film/video	Cards	Debates
Drama	**Sensory**	Discourse
Maps	Objects	Interviews
Community	Textures	Discussions
Field trips	Food	
Presentations	Models	

* Adapted from: C. Barber, *Mastery Learning Training Manual* (SE Education Service Centre, Utah p1).

Make	**Talk**	**Write**
Materials	**Verbal**	**Literary**
Diaries	Oral work	Research
Pictographs	Panels	Reports
Models	Debates	Poems
Diagrams	Brainstorms	Reviews
Items	Question/Answer	**Perform**
Drawings	**Problems**	Role plays
Presentations	Puzzles	Simulations
Films	Games	Dialogues
Tapes	Riddles	Readings

Assessment and evaluation

Just as the ship's navigator has to chart its progress according to the stated destination and keep a log of that progress, the teacher continually appraises and evaluates pupils' learning. The word evaluate means to assign worth or put a value to something. It thus includes both qualitative and quantitative approaches. The essential element is judgement which often comes as much from the teacher's wisdom as from more formal techniques of measurement.

The role of evaluation is central to the process of planning - both long- and short-term. Although much of your planned assessment procedure will be linked to the National Curriculum structure, a great deal of the day-to-day housekeeping type evaluations will not be rigidly subject to such criteria. These **formative** tools are an element of every lesson plan and should include not only the devices for measuring, evaluating and understanding the learning of your pupils but a strong administrative element in relation to the recording and reporting of the data.

When planning your lesson then, have your evaluation procedure at the forefront of your mind. It must of course never wag the tail of the teaching dog but it should help inform your planning in a way that enhances your classroom performance. Below are some common formative methods of assessment and evaluation:

Observation and sampling work

* Plan to observe as many of the pupils at work as often as you can. Begin with some predetermined criteria which will guide your observations. Or similarly set up a checklist or written guide to help you sharpen your observations.

* Take important note of the in-class tasks and activities. If oral work is to be a major element then think of possible themes that will help you understand and diagnose problems and difficulties.

* Build in as many self-monitoring and self-evaluation techniques as possible. For instance, set clear goals for particular pupils and help them evaluate their own progress. You could help this process by:

    a. Making your learning demands and objectives clear to them.
    b. Showing and indicating the rate of progress to each pupil.
    c. Pointing out weaknesses and strengths.

* Develop tests that can be administered easily and fit in with the process of classroom teaching. Such tests can be simple pencil and paper tests or involve more complex cognitive processes, e.g. problem solving or a collaborative practical experiment.

Grading and marking

No one likes being judged; no one enjoys continually being a judge. Yet the giving and receiving of grades is part and parcel of school life and is still one of the main modes of communication between teacher and pupil. When planning it is important to have an understanding of the sorts of grading systems you will use. Often this procedure is part of the department/faculty or school policy and your planning in this area should reflect this.

At the end of the Key Stage the attainment of your pupils will be systematically assessed and summarized. This assessment process will usually be **summative**. Part of this process will include teacher assessments and thus you will be required to make regular summative evaluations throughout the Key Stage. These are likely to be more formal than your formative assessments but both types of assessment are interlinked and during planning it is important to make use of both.

Homework

The key questions here are: How much? What sort? And when?

How much?
The answer here will depend on your school policy, the subject being taught and the pupils. To avoid overload, plan your homework so that it coincides with the phases of the week and corresponds with the demands of the overall curriculum. Remember to weigh up the amount of time it will take pupils to complete the task you are setting. In this sense try to individualize homework assignments as much as possible. To ensure against excessive overload have regular spot checks by asking pupils the length of time taken over particular types of homework task. In addition give homework type tasks during lessons to check the time scales involved.

What sort?

The response to this again depends on a number of variables. There are many different types of homework task that can be set so it is probably useful to think about designing homework activities that reinforce and extend existing learning. The learning of new skills and understanding is in most cases best left to the classroom where the teacher can guide and facilitate learning in a controlled way. Also, homework can be used as a basis for the following lesson. In this sense it need not always be related directly to the work just covered. Identifying new problems, finding information and exploring new ideas are all relevant to the future work of the classroom.

When?

Finally, try never to use homework as a punishment! Given the nature of pupils and schools most homework will involve pupils working independently so always try to make the tasks varied and real. The regularity of the doses must correspond to the policy of your department and school, but above all, use homework to help pupils who are struggling or those that need stretching. Planning homework is vital if you are to be successful as a teacher.

Chapter 4

The Management Stage

Introduction

Classrooms in many ways resemble other busy areas with high concentrations of people. Entering a cinema to see a popular film, waiting for a crowded train and queuing for a major sporting event all require effective management. Witness the London Underground during the rush hour when a train arrives. Often the normal rules of managed behaviour break down because the controlling procedures have come under too much strain. All too often this happens in classrooms. Thus engendering procedures, establishing routines, organizing and planning the time and space available, and preparing for the difficult transitions all help to create the right ambience. This section will examine these issues and suggest ways of effectively managing your plan.

Establishing routines

All teachers are expected to function in a manner that carries both meaning and structure for the child. The way this is enacted has been given various names, for example, essential routines, general housekeeping, etc. Such things include taking registers, distributing and collecting books and resources, keeping the learning area safe and task setting, etc.

Experienced teachers are often able to perform these standard routine activities with considerable ease and most pupils forget they are taking place at all. However, such skills have been developed over time and new teachers should take care to develop these activities early on in the school year (Leinhardt, 1983).

Teaching these routines and the rule structure that underpins them is very important and needs careful planning. In most classrooms very few rules are needed but the ones that are chosen should be inculcated and reinforced regularly. Good classroom managers are consistent in their enforcement of their planned rules and routines. These procedures are often tested during the critical phases of lessons.

These phases are usually associated with transitions from one activity to another. Researchers such as Doyle (1983) found that over 30 major transitions occur every day in classrooms and such movements make up 15 per cent of all classroom time. Such transitions include the moving of the whole class to another learning area, moving for group work, changing seating, collecting materials, moving visual aids and other equipment, etc.

These transitions must be carefully planned. A useful procedure is to adopt the step method. Here the teacher plans the broad outline of the movement, then carefully breaks down the transition into manageable bits. For instance, explaining what is going to happen, followed by who is going to move and why, where they will be moving to, what should happen after moving and the time required for the move.

Such routines are particularly important for the student or beginning teacher who needs to create their own working framework. It is vital that new entrants to the profession carefully lay down in their plans even the most mundane and obvious of procedures like distributing pencils, getting paper, choosing a book, placing equipment, etc. In addition, the planning of the seating arrangements and the orderly entry into and departure from the room, all need careful forethought. In the end the pupils will automatically come to know the rules structure and will usually act accordingly.

The guidelines below should help both beginning and experienced teachers plan these routines:

    a. Ensure that you plan the ordering of equipment, the distribution and collection of materials, etc.

    b. Try to plan to give advanced warning of transitions; flagging the event prepares the ground and helps to ease the movement.

    c. Establish early routines of entry and behaviour; plan these according to the particular class.

    d. Be consistent; follow your planned routines closely at first, especially with a new class.

Thinking about time and space

Both time and space are two areas over which teachers do have some control. Although boxed in by timetables and classroom size, teachers can still exercise a fair degree of autonomy over the use of time and the organization of their learning area.

Time

Research shows that there is a high correlation between time spent on tasks and pupil learning. Too often lesson time is seen by both teachers and pupils as something to get through - such an attitude is usually unfavourable to learning and is often associated with a lack of thought at the planning stage.

Time on task research suggests the following teacher actions which can be planned for and which may help maximize the academic and learning potential of your pupils:

* Try to diagnose accurately the ability levels of your pupils.

* Set tasks that are appropriate to their needs.

* Plan to have both substantive and substantial interaction with as many pupils as possible.

* Think about the nature of your feedback and practise appropriate dialogue.

* Plan your instructions carefully; at key points also plan reiteration thus providing reinforcement.

* Try to create an environment in which pupils are encouraged to see the intrinsic worth of the lesson.

* Try to limit the exogenous and non-substantive number of comments, particularly those related to control, and those which take the lesson off its chosen path.

Space

The way you plan for the use of classroom space can likewise have a major effect on the learning of pupils. Although desk and table arrangements have been linked to pupil behaviour and attitudes, no real firm evidence yet exists that indicates a formal relationship between desk arrangement and pupil achievement.

Some researchers have highlighted the action zone as being one of the most important areas in a classroom. This is the area which straddles the middle of the classroom. Those seated in this action zone tended to participate more in the lesson and maintained better contact with the teacher. Clearly this is related to the traditional placement of the teacher which is usually centre-front.

Such research supports the common-sense notion that the teachers' personal needs often dictate the placement of desks and tables. Weiner (1979) found that teachers with a liking for greater classroom control preferred arrangements that put them in obvious and easily communicable positions of authority.

Weinstein (1977) also found that pupils' behaviour was linked to changes in the physical layout of the classroom. Girls, it seems, avoided particular activities, and undesirable behaviour was a product of certain settings. By intervening and carefully planning the space the researchers found an improvement in both behaviour and participation.

A classic study, by Rosenfield, Lampert and Black in 1985, showed that particular seating arrangements were more conducive to particular teaching and learning strategies. For instance, they recommended that brainstorming and discussion should take place with desks arranged in circles or arches. In addition, another investigation by Kranz and Risley (1972) found that when pupils were crowded around the teacher, they were less attentive than when they were sitting in an ordered semi-circle. Finally, for more formal instruction the same researchers concluded that pupils in rows tended to withdraw more frequently, while pupils in groups tended to raise their hands more often.

Thus, when planning lessons, the arrangement of furniture should be a major consideration and could influence the overall effectiveness of the lesson. The following advice may help you in that decision-making process.

* Assess the number of chairs and tables available. Also look at the types of furniture in the classroom. Can they be moved easily? Do the tables fit

together? How quickly can they be moved?

* Link your preferred teaching style to the arrangement. Then choose how you will move the furniture to accommodate the processes you are going to use. The layout should therefore be congruent with the function.

* Carefully plan the movement. At what point in the lesson will it take place? Here you should plan the change to coincide with the most convenient point. It is always best to move desks before the lesson starts thereby minimizing disruption but this is not always possible.

Classroom formation

The formation of the classroom will serve different functions. Below are three of the most common forms of seating arrangement:

Clusters

These are commonly called groups and are usually made up of between four to six persons. They are particularly useful for small group discussions, co-operative learning and problem solving tasks, etc. Problems arise when the teacher needs to address the whole group and movement can be disruptive. Also, disparate grouping can lead to considerable off-task discussion. One possible solution is to plan the seating carefully so that you have maximum control over the situation.

Rows and columns

This is the traditional formation which is still very popular and effective. It is perhaps best used when the teacher wants the full attention of the class. However, the arrangement is not as rigid as many would have you believe and there are a number of variations. Desks/tables, for instance, could be arranged horizontally so pupils sit close to each other in fewer rows.

Circles

This formation is best for large group discussions. Do not try to have presentations or complex demonstrations unless you are sure everyone is in view and can participate.

If you are planning to have multiple resource-based activities going on simultaneously then the following guidelines may help you prepare your classroom:

* Have clearly indicated pathways to different activities. This helps to combat clashes during movement.

* Limit the number of pupils doing a particular activity. This can be problematic given the varying speeds of completion. So always plan extension material available to slow up and control queues or overuse of particular resources or activities

* Ensure pupils know where materials, etc. are stored and replaced.

* Place yourself in the best supervisory position.

Ambience

Ambience is one of those difficult concepts that appears to be a powerful factor in influencing the context of learning. Although research in this area is inconclusive, achieving the right blend and developing a pleasant working atmosphere is central to success over the long term. Two areas, namely sound and the nature of the physical environment, appear from the literature, to influence the quality of learning in classrooms.

Research has shown no direct correlation between classroom noise and achievement. A positive working buzz often indicates harmonious relations and collaborative learning. In fact when dealing with many topics pupils need to work co-operatively in order to learn new knowledge and skills. Thus we can conclude that classroom noise *per se* is not a real problem. However, certain types of noise are and these can be partly controlled by careful planning. For example, during preparation, always plan tasks so that discussion or interaction is kept to a minimum. Organize the learning area so that resources are easily available and are clearly marked. Decide on the level of acceptable noise beforehand and plan appropriate remedial actions where necessary.

Remember you do not have to be an interior designer to produce and prepare a positive classroom environment. So when preparing lessons try to create tasks that can later be displayed to give the classroom its particular feel. This approach can also serve as a useful incentive and can help develop motivation.

Motivation

Increasing, raising, developing and keeping pupils' motivation on a particular topic, theme or task is central to planning. During planning you must select and organize the lesson so that it will:

   a. Whet the pupils' appetite.
   b. Maintain their curiosity and involvement.
   c. Provide active and manipulative opportunities.
   d. Allow pupils enough choice and control over the learning without sacrificing direction.

There are a number of activities and approaches that can enhance intrinsic motivation.

* The use of challenging, positive remarks.
* The use of good illustrations.
* The introduction of personal experience.
* The setting of challenging and exploratory tasks.
* The use of creative activities.
* The careful deployment and use of anecdotes and stories.
* The introduction of games and contests.

Too often it seems classroom task structures are controlled by the use of negative forms of extrinsic motivation mostly cajoling and other authoritarian stances. When preparing lessons you can enhance the success of the lesson and reduce failure rates by following certain guidelines:

* Communicate clear instructions and expectations.
* Keep pupils on task as much as possible.
* Ensure that work is appropriate to pupils' needs and abilities.
* Give regular and prompt feedback.
* Relate past learning activities to the present.
* Develop a system of positive and frequent rewards.
* Plan your praise.
* Develop an incentive scheme that rewards without arbitrarily discriminating.

Part Three

The Plan in Action

Chapter 5

The Implementation Stage

Introduction

Implementing your plan is probably the most important and difficult phase of the planning cycle. It is here that your plan will recede into the background as your more inter-active skills begin to take over. However, the guide you have produced should be followed as closely as events will allow given that it has been designed with specific intentions in mind. In addition, in the hurly burly of the classroom, it is easy to get sidetracked and be blown off course by unplanned events. Remember your plan is based on your diagnosis of the learning capacities of your pupils. You have set your tasks, produced your resources and decided on the appropriate method - deviating heavily from your plan at this stage will put all the thinking in jeopardy.

Nevertheless, you should not let your plan handcuff you in the classroom. Usually there are two broad types of situation that can force you to deviate: firstly, when the lesson is going badly and the plan is not helping you produce the expected outcomes; secondly, when something happens just before or during the early part of the lesson that dictates necessary improvisation.

In-flight changes

Clearly it is not sensible to stick to a lesson plan that is not succeeding. For student teachers this is often a major problem for they not only lack the necessary teaching experience to decide when things are going badly but also lack the bank of personal-professional knowledge to help them replace the planned activity. During preparation then student teachers should be encouraged to develop contingency plans which can serve as reinforcements and substitutes where necessary.

Many problems of implementation are usually minor and are often associated with managing mild behaviour problems. Pupils get restless, or the class gets uneasy because of poor timing, etc. Sometimes written or practical work may be too complex or instructions unclear. These can be dealt with easily by changing focus and slipping into a new contingency-based activity. If after all that you feel a new problem is worth pursuing then leave your plan and devote your attention to the point in hand.

Of greater significance is the out-of-class problem that can make your plan obsolete or unusable. Disruption frequently occurs: messages are brought, latecomers interrupt, resources are kept too long elsewhere, etc. These have to be dealt with on the spur of the moment and you should try to minimize their effects by dealing with them briskly and quickly.

No guide book can anticipate these problems and no manual can tell you when to stick to your plan and when to deviate. These decisions must be based on your instant summing up of the problem in relation to the issues surrounding it. This form of professional knowledge is based heavily on previous case histories that help you to reflect-in-action. To gain an understanding of this process and its effects it is important to think about the changes in retrospect. Three key questions can guide your evaluation:
   a. Did the change benefit the pupils learning ?
   b. How significant was the change of course? Was it too radical a shift?
   c. Was the alternative better?

Try not to change plans capriciously. If you are suddenly inspired by a better idea during teaching try to resist it and stick to your plan. Good inspirations can work but more often than not they fail simply because they have not been fully thought through. Given this it may be useful to consider several important factors as you begin to shift from planning to performance. Even experienced teachers need to revise the following factors to ensure success in the execution of the lesson plan.

* The individual differences of your pupils.

* The length of the lesson: beginning teachers find this particularly problematic. If during a lesson you realize that too little has been planned then try to fall back on simple activities that are easily executed. For instance, quiz questions; reading out set answers, going over the main points and making summaries; discussing problems; lead into the next topic; set extension activities where necessary.
Similarly, if you have overprepared, select a point in the lesson where changes can be made. This should be of less importance than other points. Or continue the lesson, have a short conclusion and then re-plan before the next lesson, perhaps incorporating or compressing material you had planned to use.

* Be aware of the learning process and try to concentrate your energies on the pupils as learners. There is often a gap between what pupils understand and what teachers think they know and understand. This is usually related to the fact that because classrooms are so dynamic, key instances become lost in the rapidity of the movement.

When in the classroom you should always be looking for ways to improve the lesson plan. Below is a checklist which is based on current research on pupil achievement; think about the points as you organize and implement the plan in the classroom.

* Keep the lesson moving towards your stated goals.

* Keep to your schedule in terms of starting and changing activities.

* Indicate to pupils the objectives or general purpose of the lesson so they can be partners in the learning and evaluate their part in the lesson.

* Present the lesson with enthusiasm and vigour. Be brisk and 'with-it' particularly during the planned critical stages like group movements and practical experimentation.

*Explain things clearly, especially task instructions.

* Always give pupils some reflective time to think about what is being learned.

* Always check for misunderstandings.

* Elaborate on the different segments of the lesson. Make the purpose clear to the class as to the why and how of the activity.

* Try to make smooth transitions between activities and segments.

* Incorporate resources and materials into the lesson as efficiently as possible.

* Always have a lesson summary, feedback or evaluative phase at the end.

* Make sure that you highlight on your plan the important organizational elements like group set-up and make-up, homework assignments, etc.

* Listen to the pupils' comments throughout the lesson; try to store them for your post-lesson diagnosis and evaluation.

* Your initial diagnosis of your pupils' learning in relation to your planned objectives will be complemented by more complex data which you will have stored from previous classroom encounters. So, during teaching, be systematic in your observation and make notes (both mental and written) of important points about learning by individuals and the group as a whole. These may not only serve to inform your future planning but could also help if you are forced to leave your plan during the lesson because of unforeseen circumstances.

Chapter 6

The Evaluation Stage

Introduction

The evaluative stage completes the planning cycle and is in many ways the most essential aspect of the whole preparation process. It is, therefore, imperative that you plan your evaluative criteria carefully before teaching and actively consider how you are going to reflect on and judge the quality of your planning and teaching.

Broadly speaking there are three elements in the process:

Human

This covers the individuals' learning in relation to the activities set; the role of the grouping in relation to the teaching strategy adopted; and the overall cohesion of the class and the general evaluation of the learning.

Target

This centres on the achievement of the set objectives/targets bearing in mind the differentiated outcomes. The focus will obviously be as much on the nature of the tasks as on the teaching strategy used.

Context

The outcomes need to be put into perspective given the time of the lesson, the pupils' motivation, the resources available and the tempo of the day.

Evaluating and reflecting on both your script and performance is therefore crucial to your professional outlook. Learning from your successes and failures ensures the critical frame of mind so essential to the development and deployment of good teaching.

One of the most useful techniques for self-appraisal is to judge your plan and its delivery according to a set of criteria. Below is an example of some defining criteria. But remember it is probably best to develop your own in relation to each lesson or series of lessons.

* How positive are you about the lesson? Did it go well?

* In what ways was the lesson most successful/least successful?

* If you were going to teach the lesson again, what would you do differently?

* Was the plan adequate? In what ways would you change it?

* Did you achieve the overall objectives? If not where were the weaknesses? How productive was the lesson in relation to your targets?

* Was the atmosphere pleasant, workmanlike and positive?

* What sorts of misbehaviour were there? How well did you deal with them?

* How involved were the pupils? Did the group/seating arrangements work?

* Which pupils worked well? Which ones found the task difficult? What reasons can be posited for this?

* How might you help the pupils who experienced difficulties in learning?

* Were the tasks differentiated so that most pupils had access to the lesson? How can this be improved?

* Did the pupils have the same kind of opportunities to learn according to their interests and abilities?

* Was the teaching strategy congruent with the set objectives?

* How well-motivated were the pupils?

* What parts of the lesson were confusing or dull?

* Were the instructions and inputs clear?

* Were the questions appropriate and were all pupils given an equal opportunity to participate?

* How well-timed were the segments and tasks?

* What was not accomplished?

* Did you consider the abilities and interests of your pupils?

* Did you consider the pre-lesson knowledge and understanding held by your pupils?

* Were the objectives and goals appropriate to the abilities and tasks set?

* Was the lesson tied into previous ones?

* Was the lesson well-resourced given the constraints? Could the resources be improved?

* Was your teaching strategy and learning style appropriate?

* Were the activities logically developed in relation to the content of the lesson?

* Did you anticipate all the possible contingencies?

* Was the plan flexible enough for all the abilities in the class and for improvisations where necessary?

* Were your objectives attainable? How clear and concise were they?

* Would you have enjoyed the lesson if you were a pupil?

* How well-tied into the scheme of work or unit plan was the lesson?

The evaluation sheet (Figure 7) may help you think about your planning skills in relation to the stages outlined in this book.

To check the level of your understanding and ability when planning, rate yourself on the following checklist using a tick.

AREA	LEVEL		
UNDERSTANDING	HIGH	MEDIUM	LOW
My understanding of:			
Planning formats	___	___	___
The consequences of planning	___	___	___
Planning cycles	___	___	___
The role of objectives	___	___	___
The importance of Subject Matter	___	___	___
The need for a variety of teaching and learning styles	___	___	___
My ability to:			
Write appropriate objectives	___	___	___
Time segments carefully	___	___	___
Establish routines	___	___	___
Plan differentiated tasks	___	___	___
Plan the learning area	___	___	___
Plan a scheme of work	___	___	___
Design a variety of resources	___	___	___

Look carefully at the Medium and Low levels. How can you improve? What changes do you need to make in your planning?

Figure 7: Assessing your planning skills

Conclusion

Planning and Professional Development

When researching teacher planning a popular methodological tool is the process trace or thinking aloud protocol. This involves getting teachers to explain their thinking and actions as they plan and prepare lessons. This approach reveals both the complexity and intimacy of teacher planning and throws fascinating light onto their motivation, concerns and anxieties as well as on more instrumental factors such as the structure of classroom interaction, the nature of task construction, differentiation and pedagogy.

This method shows teacher planning to be not only a technical process which helps teachers organize their teaching but also a process that separates the professional elements from the purely practical. Becoming more effective planners may therefore help to breathe new life into teaching at a time when pressures for accountability are increasing. In this sense helping teachers to see these genuinely professional elements in a clearer light may further revive their commitment, improve their understanding and thereby enhance their status.

Similarly, planning and preparation are avenues by which teachers, both novice and veteran, can explore the nature of their craft and its contextual setting. This may help them understand the ways in which their practice is experienced and understood.

78

This book then, although essentially practical, is also an attempt to help practitioners step back and examine the familiar and the routine. It tries to help teachers discover the dangers of automaticity and encourages them to re-examine their professional thinking. Jerome Bruner (1960) emphasizes this very point when he talks about the need to make the familiar so strange that problematizing it becomes the essential starting point for professional regeneration. If this book helps teachers bring into consciousness even a small part of the 'hidden world' that makes up so much of their planning, then it will have served its purpose. For ultimately in the decade of the National Curriculum, schools more than ever, need 'powerful intellectuals' rather than 'minor technicians' (Smyth, 1984) to guide the learning of their pupils.

Bibliography

Assistant Masters and Mistresses Association (1991) *The Workloads of Secondary Teachers.* Warwick, University of Warwick Press.

Berieter, C., and Scardamelia, M. (1985) 'Cognitive coping strategies and the problem of inert knowledge, in S. Chapman, J. Segal and R. Glaser (eds) *Thinking and Learning Skills,* Vol. 2. Hillside, NJ, Erlbaum.

Borko, H., Livingston, C., McCaleb, J., and Mauro, L. (1988) 'Student teachers' planning and post-lesson reflections: Patterns and implications for teacher preparation.' In J. Calderhead (ed.) *Teachers' Professional Learning.* London, Falmer Press.

Broekmanns, J. (1986) 'Short term developments in student teachers' lesson planning.' *Teaching and Teacher Education,* 3(2), 215-229.

Bruner, J. (1960) *The Process of Education.* Cambridge, Mass., Harvard University Press.

Bullough, R. (1989) *First Year Teacher: A Case Study.* New York, Teachers' College Press.

Calderhead, J. (1984) *Teachers' Classroom Decision Making.* London, Holt, Reinhart and Winston.

Calderhead, J. (1988) *Teachers' Professional Learning.* Sussex, Falmer Press.

Carre, C., and Bennett, N. (1992) 'No substitute for a knowledge base.' *Times Educational Supplement.* 14 February 1992.

Carter, K. and Doyle, W. (1984) 'Variations in academic tasks in high and average ability classes.' In L. Lomas (ed.) *Classroom Research.* Victoria, Deakin University Press.

Clark, C. (1989) 'Asking the right questions about teacher education: contributions of research on teacher thinking.' In J. Lowyck and C. Clark (eds) *Teacher Thinking and Professional Action*. Leuven, Leuven University Press.

Clark, C. and Elmore, J. (1981) *Transforming Curriculum in Mathematics and Science Writing: a Case Study of Yearly Teacher Planning.* Research Series No. 99. East Lansing. Michigan, Michigan State University Press.

Clark, C. and Peterson, P. (1986) 'Teachers' thought processes'. In M. Wittrock (ed.) *Handbook of Research on Teaching.* Third edition. New York, Macmillan.

Clark, C., and Yinger, R. (1977) 'Research on teacher thinking', *Curriculum Inquiry,* 7(4), 279-394.

Clark, C. and Yinger, R. (1988) 'Teacher planning.' In J. Calderhead (ed.) *Exploring Teachers' Thinking.* London, Cassell.

Department of Education and Science (1992), 'Curriculum Organisation and Curriculum Practice in Primary Schools: A Discussion Paper'. London, DES.

Dewey, J. (1902) 'The child and the curriculum.' In J. Boyston (ed.) *John Dewey: The Middle Works 1899-1924.* Carbondale, Southern Illinois University Press.

Doyle, W. (1983) 'Academic work.' *Review of Educational Research*, 53, 159-99.

Doyle, W. (1986) 'Content representation in teachers' definitions of academic work.' *Journal of Curriculum Studies,* 18, 365-80.

Egan, K. (1989) *Teaching as Storytelling.* London, Routledge.

Gagne, R., Briggs, L. and Wager, W. (1983) *Principles of Instructional Design.* New York, Holt, Rinehart and Winston.

Grossman, P. (1987) *A passion for language: The case of Colleen, a beginning English teacher.* Knowledge Growth in a Profession Report. Stanford, CA, Stanford University Press.

Hasweh, M. (1987) 'The effects of subject matter knowledge in the teaching of biology and physics.' *Teaching and Teacher Education,* 3, 109-20.

Housner, L. and Griffey, D. (1985) 'Teacher cognition: differences in planning and interactive decision making between experienced and inexperienced teachers.' *Research Quarterly for Exercise and Sport,* 56, 45-53.

Jackson, P. (1968) *Life in Classrooms.* New York, Holt, Rinehart and Winston.

John, P. (1991) 'Course, curricular and classroom influences on the development of student teachers' lesson planning perspectives.' *Teaching and Teacher Education,* 7 (4), 359-72.

John,P. (1992) 'Knowing and understanding: the case for content knowledge in primary inset.' *British Journal of In-service Training,* 72 63-68.

John, P. (in press, 1993) 'Academic tasks in history classrooms.' *Research in Education.*

Joyce, B. and Hartootunian, B. (1964) 'Teaching as problem solving.' *Journal of Teacher Education,* 15, 420-7.

Kranz, P. and Risley, T. (1972) *The Organisation of Group Environments: Behavioural Ecology in the Classroom.* Lawrence, KA., University of Kansas Press.

Kyriacou, C. (1984) *Effective Teaching in Schools* . Oxford, Blackwell.

Kyriacou, C. (1991) *Essential Teaching Skills.* Oxford, Blackwell.

Leinhardt, G. (1983) *'Routines in expert math teachers' thoughts and judgements.'* Paper delivered at the Annual Meeting of the American Educational Research Association, Montreal.

Leinhardt, G. (1989) 'Math lesson: A contrast of novice and expert competence.' *Journal for Research in Mathematics Education,* 20, 52-75.

Leinhardt, G. and Greeno, J. (1986) 'The cognitive skill of teaching.' *Journal of Educational Psychology,* 78(2), 447-71.

MacDonald-Ross, M. (1973) 'Behavioural objectives: a critical review.' *Instructional Science, 2* (1), 1-52.

Marland, M. (1975) *The Craft of the Classroom* . London, Heinemann.

Marshall, H. and Weinstein, R. (1985) '*It's not how much brains you've got it's how you use it: A comparison of classrooms expected to enhance or undermine student self-evaluations.* ' Paper presented at the annual meeting of the American Educational Research Association, Chicago.

McDermaid, G., Ball, D. and Anderson, C. (1989) 'Why staying one chapter ahead doesn't really work: subject-specific pedagogy.' In M. C. Reynolds (ed.) *Knowledge Base for the Beginning Teacher*. Oxford, Pergamon.

McLoed, M. (1981) *''The Identification of Intended Learning Outcomes by Early Childhood Teachers: an Exploratory Study.*' Unpublished doctoral dissertation, University of Alberta.

McNamara, D. (1990) 'Subject knowledge and its application: problems and possibilities for teacher educators.' *Journal of Education for Teaching,* 17 (2), 113-128.

Ormell, C. (1992) 'Behavioural objectives revisited.' *Educational Research*, 34, 23-35.

Paine, L. (1989) *Orientation towards diversity: what do prospective teachers bring?* Research Paper No. 89. East Lansing, Michigan, Michigan State University Press.

Peterson, P., Marx, R. W. and Clark, C. (1978) 'Teacher planning, teacher behaviour and student achievement.' *American Educational Research Journal,* 15 (3), 417-432.

Popham, W. and Baker, E. (1970) *Establishing Instructional Objectives.* Englewood, NJ, Prentice-Hall.

Rosenfield, P., Lampert, N. and Black, A. (1985) 'Desk arrangement effects on pupil classroom behaviour.' *Journal of Educational Psychology,* 77,101-8.

Sardo-Brown, D. (1990) 'Experienced teachers' planning practices: A U.S. survey.' *Journal of Education for Teaching,* 16, 57-73.

Schank, A. and Abelson, T. (1977) *Scripts, Plans, Goals and Understanding.* Hilldale, NJ, Erlbaum.

School Examination and Assessment Council (1990) *Teacher Assessment in School.* London, SEAC.

Schon, D. (1984) *The Reflective Practitioner: How Professionals Think in Action.* New York, Basic Books.

Schon, D. (1987) *Educating the Reflective Practitioner: Towards a New Design for Teaching and Learning in the Professions.* San Francisco, Jossey-Bass.

Schram, P., Feiman-Nemser, S. and Ball, D. (1989) *'Think about teaching subtraction with regrouping: a comparison of beginning and experienced teachers' responses to textbooks.'* Research Paper No. 95. East Lansing, Michigan, Michigan State University.

Shulman, L. (1986) 'Those who understand: knowledge growth in teaching.' *Educational Researcher,* 15(2), 1-22.

Shulman, L. and Sykes, G. (1987) *A national board for teaching? In search of a bold standard.* Paper presented at the Task Force on Teaching as a Profession, Carnegie Forum, Stanford, Ca.

Smith, L. R. (1985) 'A low inference indication of lesson organization.' *Journal of Curriculum Organization,* 21, 25-30.

Smyth, J. (1984) 'Towards a critical consciousness in the instructional supervision of experienced teachers.' *Curriculum Inquiry,* 14, 425-436.

Stenhouse, L. (1975) *An Introduction to Curriculum Research and Development.* London, Heinemann.

Taba, R. (1956) *Curriculum Development: Theory and Practice.* New York, Harcourt.

Taylor, P. (1970) *How Teachers Plan Their Courses* . Windsor, NFER.

Taylor, P. (1975) 'A study of the concerns of students on a PGCE course.' *British Journal of*

Teacher Education, 1, 151-161.

Tyler, R. (1950) *Basic Principles of Curriculum Instructio* n. Chicago, University of Chicago Press.

Van Parraren, C. (1979) *The Action Oriented Model in the Psychology of Learning.* Brussels, University of Brussels Press.

Weick, K. E. (1979) *The Social Psychology of Organizing.* Reading, Ma. Addison-Wesley.

Weiner, B. (1979) 'The theory of motivation for some classroom experiences.' *Journal of Educational Psychology,* 71, 3-25.

Weinstein, C. S. (1977) 'Modifying student behaviour in an open classroom through changes in the physical design.' *American Educational Research Journal,* 14, 249-262.

Wilson, S., Shulman, L. and Richert, A. (1988) '150 ways of knowing: representations of knowledge in teaching.' In J. Calderhead (ed.) *Exploring Teachers' Thinking.* London, Cassell.

Wilson, S. and Wineberg, S. (1988) 'Peering at history through different lenses: the role of disciplinary perspectives in teaching history.' *Teachers College Record,* 89(4), 525-39.

Yinger, R. (1977) *'A Study of Teacher Planning: Description and Theory Development using Ethnographic and Information Processing Methods.'* Unpublished doctoral dissertation, Michigan State University.

Zahorik, J. (1970) 'The effect of planning on teaching.' *Elementary School Journal,* 71, 143-51.

Zahorik, J. (1975) 'Teachers' planning models.' *Educational Leadership,* 33, 134-9.

Index